THE GREATEST OPPORTUNITY
IN THE HISTORY OF THE WORLD

Contents

What Price Freedom?

Once upon a time, there lived a wealthy and powerful industrialist. His empire was limitless. It extended farther than the eye could see: across every ocean to every continent of the globe.

From his large, ornate mansion he controlled a vast conglomerate of successful corporations, each producing for and profiting from the others. Hundreds of thousands of people worked for him, their lives controlled by this one man. He was a master of human nature, manipulation, and control.

Although he was a private person, everything he did was in the grandest fashion. He resided in the world's most elegant mansion. He surrounded himself with great art, impeccable period furnishings, superb cuisine, vintage wines from his own vineyards and an army of servants. Everything he touched, saw, or heard was of exquisite quality.

But far and away, his most prized possession was his private zoo. It was the largest, most complete private zoo anywhere in the world. Although he had never permitted visitors, zoologists around the world envied his magnificent collection.

One day, a servant told him of a hidden valley on the Asian continent where elusive, one-of-a-kind beasts roamed. Standing atop a minaret, the industrialist watched as the animals in his zoo grazed in the open fields. These rare animals would be the perfect and final addition, he thought.

So he called his servants together and immediately assembled an expedition for the remote mountains where these rare creatures were reported to live.

He arrived at an isolated village outpost deep in the Himalayas, his quest pushing men and machines far beyond their limits. The hunters of this far corner of the world scoffed when he told them of his intention to capture the animals. They explained that no man, not even those who had lived and hunted in the valley for untold generations, could hope to capture these wild and wary creatures.

"I will return in one month," he told the villagers, "and I will capture all the animals. I ask only for a guide to show me where they are."

In one month's time he returned empty-handed. The villagers laughed and jeered at him. All he said was, "Come with me."

He took them to the high mountain meadow the guide had shown him. The village people stood and stared in shocked disbelief. There, in front of everyone were hundreds of animals held securely in a wide, fenced corral. He began to explain what he had done.

On the first morning, he set out a ration of rich sweet-feed and a bale of hay in the center of the meadow. He went again the next day, and the next, each day setting out new feed and hay. Soon the animals came and ate. Only a few at first, but every day more would come. Eventually, the entire herd was eating at the meadow.

Then in the evenings, he dug holes for fence posts, setting two or three posts every night. When the circle of posts was complete, he began placing the rails. He started with those lowest to the ground, which were easy for the animals to step over. Each evening he added a new rail to the fence, building each side of the corral higher and higher as the days went by. Finally the animals could only enter and leave through a small opening in the fence.

On the evening of the 29th day, he constructed a gate. On the last day, after all the animals had walked through the narrow opening, he closed the gate behind them and locked it. Before those beautiful and free creatures realized what had happened, they were trapped.

He told the amazed villagers, "I can capture any animal by simply having it depend on me for its food. I can control any person the same way. It is a fair exchange, really. I feed them, they give me their beauty and their freedom. That is the source of my wealth and my power."

Do You Sometimes Feel Trapped?

How many of us feel trapped by our dependence on someone or something outside of ourselves for our sweet-feed?

How many of us have become prisoners of a manipulative system that was erected so subtly—one post, one rail at a time—only to awaken to the realization that we were fenced in and that the gate to our futures was locked and barred?

How many of us are living in a perpetual state of survival?

I wish I had a nickel from every person I met who told me that they didn't like what they did for a living. "I hate my job; I hate my boss; I hate my environment and I hate the traffic I have to fight five days a week to get to and from all these things I hate."

Many of us are so caught up with keeping up that survival is all we see and focus on. We're so concerned with making a living that we forget how to truly live. I guess it says a lot for the resiliency of the human spirit. It's amazing that so many of us will tolerate so much pain—just to survive. Especially when it's so unnecessary.

I wish I had a dollar from every person with a better-than-average income, who recognizes the subtle fences being erected around them as a direct result of their prosperity. Many of the responsibilities that come with financial success can keep us from our once "pure idea" of freedom, just as surely as if we were encircled by barbed wire. Does financial success have any meaningful value if we feel that it has taken control of our lives?

A BETTER WAY

My friends, there is a better way to work and live. There is a way to leave behind the constant focus on survival, and to regain creative control of your life.

There is a way to be free!

I have tried many "better ways." Although they were all interesting and each offered its own unique opportunity for learning and enjoyment, there is only one that fulfills its own broad promise. It can offer you extraordinary freedom of choice, unlimited possibilities for the highest imaginable success in every aspect of your work and life, and the ability to fully and completely, once and for all, take control of your life. To actually be, do and have all you ever wanted.

That "new and better way" is what this little book is all about.

I call it *The Greatest Opportunity in the History of the World*.

CHAPTER TWO

Your Magic Carpet

What if this book revealed to you a magic carpet
that could lift you over all your fences
and whiz you through the air,
to health and wealth and happiness,
if you just tell it where.

Would you let it take you
where you've never gone before,
or would you buy some drapes to match
*and use it on your floor?**
— Shel Silverstein

Which would you do?

The answer isn't as obvious as it may seem.

---

* Shel Silverstein, A Light in the Attic (Harper and Row, 1981)

7

I meet thousands of people in my talks and seminars, and they fall into two distinct groups: those who believe that anything is possible and those who do not. Those who believe in magic carpets, and those who see only a rug lying on the floor.

What do you see? If you see a rug, all you may need is a paradigm shift.

SHIFTING YOUR PARADIGMS

Listen to this story told by Stephen Covey in his book, *The Seven Habits of Highly Effective People.*

One dark and stormy night, two battleships were returning to port after a training mission. The seas were heavy and the patchy fog made visibility very poor, so the captain remained on the bridge to make sure all went well.

Shortly after dark, the lookout reported, "Light bearing off the starboard bow."

"Is she steady or moving astern?" the captain asked.

"Steady, captain," the lookout replied, which meant the ship was on a collision course!

The captain ordered the signalman, "Signal that ship: 'We are on a collision course, advise you change course 20 degrees.'"

Back came a signal, "Advise *you* change course 20 degrees."

The captain said, "Send this: 'I am a captain, change course 20 degrees.'"

Back came the reply, "I am a seaman second class, advise *you* change course 20 degrees."

The captain, now quite irate, barked back the command, "I am a *battleship*. Change course 20 degrees!"

Back came the flashing signal. "I am a lighthouse." *

That's a paradigm shift!

That one small bit of information, "I am a lighthouse," instantly changed the captain's point of view. You could say that he became wide open to a new way of looking at things.

I CHALLENGE YOU TO BE OPEN

So, I'm going to challenge those of you who see just a rug on the floor to be open to the possibility that it's not what you thought at first. That it may be a magic carpet which actually can take you "where you've never gone before."

---

* Stephen R. Covey, *The Seven Habits of Highly Effective People* (New York: Simon Schuster, 1989).

I'm challenging you, the captain of your own ship of fate, to see this book as a lighthouse, to accept the "enlightenment" that's shining out at you from these pages.

Why should you?

Great question!

Well, if you think about it, you have nothing to lose. If you don't find a "magic carpet of opportunity" in this book, no harm done. But if the greatest opportunity in the history of the world *actually can* take you to a whole new life of "health, wealth and happiness…" well, that's worth the effort of imagining it's truly possible. Wouldn't you agree?

Knowledge is power. Armed with that power, you'll be able to pick out magic carpets anywhere. To do that, though, you have to be open, and willing to see things in a different light.

Think of something, right now, that you believe you can do. Anything is fine: mowing the lawn, writing your name, playing the piano. So, why do you believe you can do it? *Because you've done it.* You *know* you can do it.

That's easy. Now try this. How do you come to believe that you can do something that you've *never done before?*

For starters, you may build up some quantity of knowledge that shows you it *can* be done. And you get that from other people who have already done it successfully. As you watch and listen to them describe how it's done, you come to understand and believe that it's possible for you, too.

John Ruskin, a 19th century British writer, describes this process beautifully. I'd like to share it with you.

"The greatest thing a human soul ever does in this world is to see something and tell what he saw in a plain way. Hundreds of people can talk for one who can think, and thousands can think for one who can see. To see clearly is poetry, prophecy and religion all in one."

JIM'S STORY

As a modern-day example of a person who tells plainly what he sees, here's Jim's story.

I was presenting a training seminar a few years ago. There was a young man there named Jim. I noticed Jim because he was one of the first people to arrive and the very last to leave. He was personable and friendly—a really nice guy.

By talking with Jim and asking him a few questions, I quickly learned that the most important thing in his life was his family. He pulled out pictures of his wife and children. He just glowed with pride as he told me all about them.

Although he was very loyal and did his work diligently, Jim wasn't happy. Like many people in the world, Jim didn't like his job. He did it, he said, because he needed the money to provide for his family.

I learned other things about Jim. I mostly learned how afraid he was. Jim wanted more than anything in the world to go out on his own and start his own business. He thought of himself as smart and creative.

What stopped Jim was fear.

He was afraid of failing, afraid of what others would think if he didn't succeed. He was scared to risk striking out on his own, putting his family's finances in jeopardy if it didn't work out. He was afraid of losing his home, his security, his sense of self-esteem and self-worth. What's more, he was convinced that's exactly what he would do: Fail.

Jim knew of the opportunities that Network Marketing provided. But he had tried it before, and it didn't work out for him like he expected. Consequently, he had a "doubting" belief system. One failure and he was convinced the system was not for him.

As he left that evening, I had a deep sense of compassion for Jim. Here was a tremendous guy, with all the talent he'd ever need to be a great success, *fenced in* by his fears and doubts. What Jim lacked was a magic carpet that could lift him over the fences of his fears and on to the success he so richly wanted and truly deserved.

A couple of weeks later, I got a phone call from Jim. Something had happened to him he wanted to share.

He had just come back from the funeral of a very dear friend of his, a man he grew up with and loved very much. As he was sitting in the room looking at the coffin, he began to reflect on his friend's life.

"He was a truly wonderful man," Jim said. "So talented, caring and full of splendid ideas and big dreams. But something always seemed to get in his way. Without fail, for one reason or another, he never did what he said he'd do and what he dreamed of doing. All of a sudden, it hit me, John. This could be *my* funeral. That could be *me* in that coffin, with *my* family and *my* friends thinking the same of me."

Needless to say, that really shook Jim up.

"John, right then and there I decided that *was not* going to happen to me! I wasn't going to be that guy in the coffin with my friends thinking I never even tried! John, I'm gonna go for it, right now. This very minute!"

Well, I didn't hear from Jim again for about a year. One day, out of the blue, he called. He wasn't sure if I remembered him—but I did.

"John, I just had to call and tell you all about what's been happening to me. My life immediately started changing the very moment I made that commitment over a year ago. It's incredible!

"You know, as long as I can remember I've wanted to drive a brand-new Mercedes. Well, guess what I'm driving now? And remember how I told you my wife and I always wanted to dress like a million? We just love fine clothes and how they make us feel. Well, you should see us now! We're also moving into our new home next month, John, and in the meantime, I'm taking Karen and the kids to Hawaii for a two-week vacation. I'll tell ya, it just doesn't get much better than this!"

And then Jim's voice changed. He became a little less bubbly, a bit more reserved. It made me wonder what he was going to say next.

"John, I found that magic carpet, just like you said I would. But it's so much better than I ever imagined. I finally have my own Network Marketing business. I love the products we market, they really work and the company has some great people behind it! They really know what they're doing."

"The people in my network are just fantastic! I've never met more interesting and supportive people in my life! And they look to me as their leader! It's true, I'm training people just like you taught me—and I'm very, very good at it. I have the fastest-growing Network within my company, and I'm having a ball."

Then, Jim's voice changed again. It got deeper and even more thoughtful and serious. "Now what?" I wondered.

"And John, even more importantly, I feel like I've found myself and have come home. There's no difference anymore between my life and my work. They're the same thing. My wife and kids are so proud of me. You know, John, my wife and I are the only parents that always show up for every little league game. The only ones! Talk about 'quality time.' All my time is quality time now—and because of it, my kids think I'm a hero!

"My wife and I... well, we always wanted to spend more time together. So now we're working the business together! She's doing great, and loving every minute of it! It's a total family business now. Even the kids enjoy helping out any way they can. Everything is so special, it's hard for me to believe it's all happening.

"John, I can't begin to tell you how all this makes me feel. It's absolutely the best. I feel I am making a positive difference in the lives of hundreds, maybe even thousands, of people. It's a great feeling, it's a great gift!

"And John, I just can't thank you enough for helping me get started in all of this. It is the greatest opportunity in the history of the world. Thank you. Thank you so very much."

Whew! After I hung up the phone with Jim, I sat back, dried my eyes, cleared my throat and took a big, long deep breath.

"The greatest opportunity in the history of the world," Jim had said. Well, I guess so! What a changed

---

man he was! And what a thrill it was to listen to him and share in his success.

By simply shifting his paradigm—from rug to magic carpet—Jim was able to see things differently. And that new picture was all he needed to *do* things differently. He changed his thinking, which changed his life. And it all happened because he was willing to be open.

BE, DO, HAVE

Did you notice in Jim's story that he started out by telling me about all the things he had? Then he told me about what he was doing. And he ended up talking about who he had become.

Have, do, be. It fascinates me that in all my years of training and giving seminars, most people say it that way: *Backwards.* People think we need to *have* certain things, whether it's looks, outstanding talent, money or extraordinary skills, before we can *do* what we want, and only then will we *be* who we'd like to be.

That's not how it works. We *have* what we want because we *do* what it takes to get it. We *do* what it takes because we are *being* the kind of person who does those kinds of things. *Be, do, have.* That's really the way it works.

We aren't human *havings* or human *doings*. We're human *beings*!

It's just like "seeing is believing." We've got that backwards, too. Believing is *seeing*. We see what we believe. Nothing more, nothing less. And until we believe we can have something in our life, we won't see it!

Take Jim, for example. Until he believed it was possible to be what he truly wanted, he couldn't see any hope. At his friend's funeral, he learned a very powerful lesson about what *he didn't* want to be. That's when he knew, beyond a shadow of a doubt, that he had to be a success. That's when he made the *commitment* to go for it. And that's when things started to happen *as if by magic*.

If you haven't already, I challenge you to make that same commitment right now. Make the choice to live your dreams and refuse to settle for anything less than what you want! When you do, "all manner of unforeseen incidents and meetings and material assistance..." will come your way.

WHEN THE STUDENT IS READY

Have you ever heard, "When the student is ready, the teacher appears?"

Well, my friends, the teacher in me is *ready*! It's part of my job and my life's purpose to share this information with you.

Is the student in you ready?

TEA FOR TWO

In ancient Japan, it was the custom for a student seeking admission to study at a monastery to have an audience with the master. As was tradition at these interviews, the master would serve tea.

One day, a highly-intelligent and most accomplished young student approached the master for such a meeting. As they sat together, the young man enthusiastically told the master of his knowledge and accomplishments.

When the master offered tea, the student consented and without missing a beat continued speaking.

All of a sudden he jumped up, startled by the tea flooding over the table top and down onto his legs.

"Master, the cup is full to overflowing!" he exclaimed. The master continued to pour, the tea spilling out onto the table and floor.

"As are you," the master replied. "Please, come back and see me when you are empty and more in need of my teaching."

Now don't get me wrong. I'm far from being the expert or master here. I'm just a simple person, much like you, who is actively pursuing the path of understanding and mastery. The moment I start to believe I've learned all there is to learn, I think of the master with his tea kettle. That's when I realize how little I do know.

I *may* be a little further along the path of understanding than you—*and maybe not*. Either way, I am more than willing to share with you what I've learned so far. After reading this book, you may choose a different path—and believe me, that's OK. I've discovered that by sharing with you what I am learning, I move further along my own path, no matter what you choose to do with what I share.

FOR ONE TO LEARN, ONE MUST FIRST BE OPEN

The Zen masters call the state of being open to all around you "The Beginner's Mind." It's a state-of-mind where you see things with freshness and wonder, like a child.

No, I'm not asking you to act naive or to ignore the truth. Quite the opposite. What I am saying is that once you see Network Marketing with a beginner's mind, no matter what you've previously experienced or heard, you will see it for what it really is and you'll experience a tangible sense of hope. And hope, my friends, is something we could all use more of!

TO WALK AMONG GIANTS

Some of you may also have preconceived notions about the content of this book, based upon your opinion of the person who gave it to you. Perhaps you think you're already more successful than that person. Maybe you think you're smarter than they are.

Well, that's great! Good for you and good for them!

David Ogilvy, the famous guru of Madison Avenue, built the highly-successful worldwide advertising agency Ogilvy & Mather. Whenever he appointed someone to run one of his new offices, he would send them a set of nesting Russian dolls. You know the kind, where you take one apart, and inside, there's another, slightly smaller one, and another, and so on. Inside the last, littlest doll was a piece of paper that said:

"If each of us hires people who are smaller than we are, we shall become a company of dwarfs, but if each of us hires people who are bigger than we are, Ogilvy & Mather shall become a company of giants."

So, if you feel you are smarter or more successful than the person who gave you this book, congratulations to the both of you.

IT'S TIME TO ASK YOURSELF...

"Am I open to the possibility that the rug over there can truly be a magic carpet?"

If you're not, that's okay. I understand. And there's really no point in your reading any further. Give this book back to the person who gave it to you, or pass it on to someone who might be more interested. Perhaps some time in the future will be better for you. I'm not here to try and convince you. My purpose is simply to share this information with as much integrity and enthusiasm as I can.

Now, if you are open yet skeptical, that's great! That lets me know that you're a thoughtful person—willing to be persuaded by the truth. And I want you to know something else. As a reader, you are a volunteer. You don't have to do anything! I'll just lay out the facts and you can make an educated choice. Fair enough?

And, if you're sitting there chomping at the bit, saying to yourself, "Come on John, come on, I'm ready already, let's get to the good stuff!"

Fantastic! I'm ready too!

So, let's get started. I promise to show you that this rug is truly a magic carpet. Why is that so? Because it's...

The Greatest Opportunity In The History Of The World!

CHAPTER THREE

What Is The Greatest Opportunity In The History Of The World?

As you may have guessed, the greatest opportunity in the history of the world is Network Marketing.

When I talk about Network Marketing, I'm including companies with multi-level, or MLM structures and even a few direct-selling companies. Since "Network Marketing" is the more progressive name, I'll use it from now on to describe this young and explosive industry.

The first time I was exposed to Network Marketing, over fourteen years ago, I was so excited I couldn't sleep. I laid in bed all night, wide-awake and thinking of

23

all the possibilities this new concept could bring. I sensed then that this wonderful industry would be a part of my life forever.

The next morning, I set a goal to help myself make the most of this new and amazing opportunity. *Before I die*, I told myself, *I want to have one million friends.* That's my goal! So everything I do is centered around building new, quality relationships.

That goal is also the reason for our company's name, Millionaires In Motion. Although my team and I are deeply committed to this industry, we have no financial interest in any Network Marketing company or product.

We direct our efforts to providing educational programs and tools to help support *all* Network Marketing entrepreneurs in their pursuit of excellence. So, my friend, I know of no better way to serve you than to introduce you to Network Marketing itself. That's my product—my only product!

One of the keys to this business is loving your product. Successful Network Marketers love their products so much that they'll enthusiastically recommend them to anyone, anywhere, anytime. Well, I'm just as passionate about my product too. Network Marketing is the wave of the future. And I'm convinced that one way or another, this industry is going to be a part of *your* future too.

NETWORKING AND MARKETING

John Fogg, my good friend and editor of the highly-respected industry newsletter *Upline™* says, "Network Marketing is the next logical step in the evolution of the free enterprise system." The reason? It combines two of the most powerful forces at work in our world today: Networking and Marketing.

For me, a great example of networking is the story of Craig Shergold, a little nine-year-old boy from England with a life-threatening brain tumor. After doctors diagnosed his condition, they gave him little hope of recovering. Craig's only wish was to be mentioned in the *Guinness Book of World Records* for receiving the most get-well cards in history.

Well, a number of newspapers picked up the story and in a few short weeks, Craig had received hundreds of cards. One person in the United States learned of the boy's challenge and put the request out over a computer bulletin board that *networked* with people around the world. Within only six months, Craig had received nine million get-well cards! Two years later, he had received 27 million cards.

That is the extraordinary power of Networking.

Now, what about Marketing?

According to *USA Today*, the United States alone marketed $5.5 trillion worth of goods and services in

1990. Need I say more about the effectiveness of marketing?

Combining these two powerful systems produces an awesome force for distributing goods and services. That's why Network Marketing has been called "the wave of the future."

Now perhaps you know somebody who has a poor opinion of Network Marketing. You may have heard someone say Network Marketing was ethically questionable or illegal. Let's put this misinformation to rest right now.

WHAT NETWORK MARKETING *IS NOT*

1. Network Marketing IS NOT an illegal "pyramid scam." It is not a chain letter or illegal lottery where people make money by recruiting others to join in the game. Network Marketers are paid *only* on the distribution of valuable products or services. I'll explain this later in more detail.

2. Network Marketing IS NOT a "get-rich-quick" business. Although fast money has happened for a few individuals, they are rare exceptions, not the rule. But if you drop the "quick" and call it a "get-rich" business, that's another matter.

3. Network Marketing IS NOT just for professional salespeople. Of the countless success stories in the industry, most have come from individuals with non-sales backgrounds and little or no experience.

4. Network Marketing IS NOT a full-time commitment.

Nearly ninety percent of the men and women in this industry work their business part-time.

5. Network Marketing IS NOT for men only. Actually, the majority of active, successful people in the industry are women. I'll invest more time on this fascinating fact a little later.

Unfortunately, Network Marketing IS misunderstood by most of the general public. There are those who have had an unfortunate experience of one kind or another. Others, because of what they've heard, think it's an "illegal pyramid." But as Dr. Dean Black, author of "The MLM Simple Success Guide" says, "There's nothing wrong with the principle, just with the way some people work with it."

The truth is it's legal and it works! And it's working for a lot of people who have learned how to make it work for them.

NETWORK MARKETING
AND RESIDUAL INCOME

If you're like most people, you probably earn your income in one of three ways.

1. You can be an employee. This is what most people do, whether they're paid by the hour, by commission, or by a salary. Either way, with the exception of some paid holidays and vacations, you only earn money when *you* do the work. And it's an accepted fact that most employees, no matter how good they are, can only earn a maximum of twenty-five percent of their true value. The company needs the rest to operate the business.

This is called having a job. Have you ever heard motivational speaker Zig Ziglar say what the word "job" stands for? Just **O**ver **B**roke!

2. You can own your own business. Ah, the ultimate dream. Truth is, for most people, it's more like a nightmare! According to the Small Business Administration, ninety percent of all small businesses fail in the first two years. Of those that make it, eighty percent of *them* will fail within the next five. How many businesses do you know that are ten years old? Or twenty? And as most small business owners will tell you, their business really owns *them*. Seventy- to eighty-hour work weeks are all too common for these busy entrepreneurs. Many of them actually own their own *jobs*.

3. You can earn income from your investments. It's true that you can earn $5,000 a month or more from wise investments of your capital. The challenge is, you've got to have a small fortune to start with. About $500,000 to $750,000 will yield the kind of income you want from stocks and bonds, CDs or real estate. Most people don't have that kind of money.

There is another way of earning money. Inventors, singers, writers and actors have known this for years. It's called *residual income*. Basically, this allows you to earn from your initial efforts even though you are no longer directly involved on a day-to-day basis. It's like the royalties a singer receives on an album which continues to sell. This is the kind of income Network Marketing offers. Sound interesting?

Here's how it works.

The first step is to choose a Network Marketing company: one with products that you think are fantastic, management you respect and trust, and a solid business development program. A little later in the book I'll give you some ideas on what to look for in a Network Marketing company.

You begin by using the products yourself and sharing them with your family and friends, just as you would with a good movie or a book you enjoyed. We call that *consumer advocacy*. With Network Marketing, however, each time you recommend a product you receive a retail commission.

Gradually, as you share the products with others, you'll find a number of people interested in the business opportunity—just like you. You then sponsor these people by working with them, training and helping them build Networks of their own. For each person you sponsor, you receive a commission on each sale that they, and everyone in *their* networks, produce.

In twelve to forty-eight months, you can build a business that actually earns $5,000 to $10,000 or more in monthly residual income. The best part is that you don't have to show up every day to continue to earn those commissions. Beats punching a time clock, doesn't it?

WHAT NETWORK MARKETING *IS:*

The following is a laundry list of hard and soft facts about Network Marketing:

1. Network Marketing IS open to everyone of legal age—regardless of sex, education, race, religion, business experience, social standing, past successes or failures.

2. Network Marketing IS a legal and ethical business structure. It is recognized in Canada, the United Kingdom, Australasia, Germany, Japan, Malaysia and many other countries throughout the world. In the United States, it is recognized and regulated by the Federal Trade Commission (FTC), the IRS, and other state and federal agencies.

3. Although no precise figures exist (because most companies in the industry are privately held and are not required to publish their financial statements), experts believe Network Marketing IS currently at a level of approximately $15 to $25 billion in annual sales. If you include direct sales companies who market their products or services through Network Marketing divisions or subsidiaries, that figure could

top $50 billion! Some of these companies include Colgate-Palmolive, Gillette, MCI and US Sprint.

4. Some U.S. Network Marketing companies are also on the New York Stock Exchange and Fortune's list of 100 Fastest Growing Companies. A few examples are Avon, Shaklee, Amway, A.L. Williams (now Primerica), and Mary Kay Cosmetics.

5. In Network Marketing, you own your own business. You are the boss!

6. In Network Marketing you are a volunteer. You're under *no obligation* to do anything.

7. In Network Marketing, you can typically begin your business for as little as twenty dollars and up to a few hundred dollars. This money goes towards a distributor kit, sales support material and initial product inventory. And most, if not all, of your investment is usually guaranteed.

8. Network Marketing IS a professional career opportunity. Because so many people are involved in it part-time, you might think it's a kind of money-making hobby. However, one look at the number of professionals and white-collar men and women entering the industry will change your opinion. We'll talk more about this later, too!

9. There is no need to employ high-pressure sales tactics and manipulative closing techniques. Network

Marketing IS a "sorting" business based on finding the right people who fit with you, your product and your opportunity.

10. Network Marketing IS all about freedom of choice. You are free to choose who, when, where, why, and how you operate your business. Network Marketing puts *you* in control of your life.

THE TURN-KEY REVOLUTION

I've always been interested in the Japanese, their philosophy and language. They have a character which I think adequately describes the evolution of our business world. In Japanese, the character *kaizen* represents "gradual improvements over time." Over the years, we have been looking for more effective and less costly ways of doing business, gradually improving on the method that had existed before.

For instance, franchising used to be the "crown prince" of free enterprise. When it began over thirty years ago, hardly anyone had heard of the concept. Now, with more than $750 billion in annual sales of goods and services, franchising has become a part of our life-style. Our appetite for hamburgers alone has helped McDonalds become the industry leader, with well over $60 billion in annual sales.

Franchising is still a phenomenal concept. Anyone

who wants to own their own business can do so, without consuming time and money in research and development. The parent company will provide all of that. All you need to do is walk in and turn the key. Because of this, franchises are also called "turn-key operations."

But there's a catch. The average start-up cost for a franchise is about $85,000. Ouch!

So why is Network Marketing the logical next step?

Network Marketing gives you all the benefits of a franchise for a fraction of a fraction of the cost!

What's more, a successful Network Marketer has a far better chance of earning as much, if not more, than a franchisee. How? Residual income.

So, how do you build a successful Network Marketing business of your own?

I explain all of that in my book *Being The Best You Can Be In MLM*. I'm very proud of *Being The Best*, and very gratified that so many industry experts uphold it as "the best 'how-to' book there is on Network Marketing." I promise you that reading that book will take you step-by-step through all you need to know to start and build a tremendously successful Networking business. So, if you have questions about "how to," get a copy of my book and learn all about it.

For now, I want you to have the kind of knowledge

and understanding about Network Marketing that you'll need to establish a one hundred percent unshakable faith in this industry. I want you to be able to see the "magic carpet" it's offering you. I want you to see that this truly *is* the greatest opportunity in the history of the world!

The best way to do that is a history lesson.

Come on now, no groans. I know most of us think that history wasn't interesting and fun in school. But it can be. For example, did you see the movie *Dances With Wolves*?

My wife Yvonne and I went to see it. I didn't have any expectation for the film going in. I just heard it was good, and my friends said I should see it.

Well "good" was clearly not good enough. What an exceptional film! When it was over and the credits were rolling, Yvonne and I sat transfixed, glued to our seats. The tears welled up in my eyes. There was a knot in my chest and an empty, almost longing sensation in my stomach.

My heart was aching for the Native Americans. My head was filled with a flood of images washing over each other: their nobility, their wisdom, the simple grace of how they lived, how they related to the animals, the land, each other.

I've seen many "cowboy and Indian" movies before,

many of which were entertaining. But I do not remember being so touched, so physically moved as I was that night. I guess that's why they call them movies. They're made to *move* you!

That film was a "lighthouse" for me. It changed the way I looked at American history—my history!

Now, I don't claim to be as talented as award winning actor/director Kevin Costner, and I don't pretend that the birth and development of Network Marketing will be as moving for you as *Dances With Wolves* was for Yvonne and me. But I can promise you this: When you understand this business, and when you believe that it holds the possibility to take creative control of your life and to establish for yourself a rock-solid foundation of financial and personal freedom, your life may never be the same again!

So, let's quickly look back over the past fifty years and discover how Network Marketing was born and grew to where it is today. After all, we can't know where we're headed unless we know where we've been.

The Birth Of An Industry

Since its inception, Network Marketing has grown far beyond the creative and geographical boundaries of just one country. In fact, as an American who travels the world and speaks internationally with people in the industry, I can comfortably say that there is a growing number of people and cultures who understand and embrace the power of Network Marketing—some even more than Americans.

The concept of Network Marketing, however, was born in the United States, so you will notice that much of the industry's past is deeply rooted in American history.

To the best of my knowledge, the first company to

enter the Network Marketing industry was California Vitamins back in the early 1940s.

They were the first because at that time they were the only business that incorporated a sales and compensation program with a number of different levels. Hence the term "multi-level."

Although there were many direct sales companies like the travelling housewares stores and Fuller Brush men, California Vitamins enabled its representatives to sponsor other people into the business and earn commissions from the sales of these people as well. It was an independent organization where the sales people themselves, rather than the company, hired, trained and managed their own sales force. In essence, each person had the opportunity to build his or her own sales organization with the company providing products and paying commission checks.

After a few years, the company changed its name to Nutrilite. Two of the company's star distributors, Rich DeVos and his lifelong friend Jay Van Andel, caught the vision of what was possible with this new Multi-level Marketing concept. For them, it was the perfect way to bring the American dream to an unlimited number of people. In 1959, DeVos and Van Andel broke away from Nutrilite to found their own Multi-level Marketing (MLM) company, the Amway Corporation. Amway is taken from the two words "American Way."

As of 1993, Amway is a $5 billion, multi-national cor-
poration with over two million independent representatives worldwide. Talk about a powerful vision!

A BOOMING BUSINESS?
NOT YET...

The industry developed slowly from 1959 to 1975. At
that time, only thirty firms could be called *true* Multi-
level Marketing companies. (The term Network Marketing was not used back then.)

Yet by the late 1960s, the efforts of one man, Glen
Turner, would soon change all that, partly for the better
and partly for the worse.

Back then, Glen Turner was like the "Pied Piper."
Many believed he could charm the moon out of the sky
and bring rocks to life. His vision of success and personal achievement was a siren's song to men and
women from every walk of life. He offered people a new
life by convincing them that anything was possible.

He founded Glen W. Turner Enterprises, which was a
collection of smaller companies with a variety of products that quickly took the country by storm. Two of his
most successful enterprises were Koscot Interplanetary
Incorporated and Dare To Be Great.

Thousands and thousands of people flocked to Mr.
Turner and his opportunity. What he had to say about

human potential and achieving success was right on. Even today, people are still using his concepts of training and motivation. He was a master at bringing out the best in people, and there are many, many people today who owe their success to his teaching and inspiration.

Unfortunately, Turner Enterprises was also credited with something else: the perfection of the "illegal pyramid scheme." Some of the products sold were either questionable or never existed. The real money for the Turner Enterprise distributors came from recruiting others.

Since there weren't any laws or restrictions governing Multi-level Marketing at the time (remember it was still in its infancy), Glen W. Turner Enterprises was allowed to continue. Later, however, he was convicted and served a seven-year prison sentence.

The first real crackdown on the Multi-level Marketing industry *itself* actually started in 1975. As it turns out, this became the catalyst for a tidal wave of sustained growth which continues to this day.

Acting on rumors of illegal distribution, the United States Federal Trade Commission (FTC) attacked the Multi-level Marketing industry with what we now know as the "Pyramid Laws." Of the thirty companies existing at the time, Amway took on the brunt of the challenge. After investing four long years and $4 million of their money in court costs, Amway's battle with the FTC ended.

In what we refer to today as the Amway decision (FTC vs. Amway 93 FTC 618), the court ruled that Amway was *not* an illegal pyramid and that its method of distribution (Multi-level Marketing) was a viable and legitimate channel for sales and distribution of products.

I feel that the key to the industry's survival back then was Amway's willingness to take a stand for what they believed was right. Had it not been for their commitment, the greatest opportunity in the history of the world wouldn't exist today.

I, for one, am eternally grateful. Thanks a million, Amway!

BUILDING THE GREAT PYRAMIDS

For four long years, entrepreneurs waited on the safety of the sidelines as Amway, the industry champion, battled for its survival and theirs. Once the way was clear, small business developers of every conceivable intent entered the fray. The window of opportunity was now wide open.

Although many fine companies were formed during this explosion, many not-so-fine enterprises began as well. Among them were a number of what we know today as "pyramid scams."

What do we know about pyramids? A pyramid is the most enduring physical structure we know of. With its broad foundation, a pyramid can grow to great heights and yet remain solid and stable. Dr. Dean Black, in his wonderful booklet *The MLM Simple Success Guide,* describes a pyramid as follows:

"Above a certain size any organization that distributes products or services ends up shaped like a pyramid, with multiple levels that get bigger as you go down. Delegation creates a multi-level pyramid. Our government is also a multi-level pyramid. So are our schools and churches. All successful businesses, because they distribute products and services, end up shaped like a pyramid."

Dean Black goes on to explain a most important point I want you to understand—that the power in any multi-level pyramid structure comes from the bottom. Here's how he describes it:

"Our government distributes services down a pyramid, but we give it power from the bottom, with our votes. Marketing companies distribute products down a pyramid, but we give them power from the bottom with our dollars. So pyramids set up a flow that runs two ways: first down then up. Value flows down the pyramid; power, in response, flows up. If value stops flowing down, power (in the form of dollars or votes) stops flowing up, and the system collapses." *

---

* K. Dean Black, Ph.D., "The MLM Simple Success Guide" (Brerie Enterprises, Springville, UT.).

So it's not a question of whether or not something is structured like a pyramid. There's nothing inherently wrong with the pyramid structure. It's a question of *value*. And it's the lack of value that makes any business enterprise morally, ethically or legally questionable.

When a business enterprise does not provide real value, whether it's conventional or multi-level, it's called a *scam*. A *scam* is a fraudulent business scheme or swindle. Does the word "scamp" ring a bell? A scamp is a highway robber, a street ruffian, or a rogue.

So a "pyramid" is actually a good method for distributing products and services and a "pyramid scam" is highway robbery disguised as a legitimate multi-level structure.

No matter what we call it, the law is clear. Legitimate Multi-level or Network Marketing *is* a viable system of distribution and sales where independent contractors earn commissions on the sales of products from a manufacturer or marketer to the end consumer. *The one and only way to earn money in this business is from the sales of products.* As we have seen in the past, being paid for the mere act of recruiting is a scam, no matter what shape or form it's packaged in.

Here's a simple way for you to test any MLM/Network Marketing opportunity. *If someone earns a commission from the registration fee you would pay to join the company as a distributor, more than likely it's illegal!*

People are being compensated on recruiting you as a member. They should only earn commissions on the products or services you purchase and distribute.

THE NETWORK MARKETING PHENOMENON

Between 1979 and 1983 (after the Amway decision), over *5 million* men and women joined the industry. Hundreds and hundreds of companies emerged within that short period. It was an entrepreneurial free-for-all, a frenzied time for the industry and everyone involved.

Many of the companies that developed during this period, were of the "Mom n' Pop" variety. They began in basements, garages and spare rooms. Anyone with a unique idea for a product and a dream of great success could enter the industry with the hope of achieving their dreams. Under-capitalized and under-experienced, they came and went at an alarming rate.

Network Marketing has long suffered the reputation of having a greater corporate failure rate than other conventional small business enterprises. It's not true. These Mom n' Pop companies—which began from a few well-intentioned people suffering from entrepreneurial seizures—never really had much of a chance. The industry at that time was filled with everything from honest ignorance to unprofessionalism and yes, even outright fraud: mostly, though, just honest ignorance! Yet a few good companies did emerge, and some of these companies are the leaders in the Network Marketing industry today.

More importantly, hundreds of thousands of people caught the vision of a new and better way to live and work as independent Network Marketing distributors. These folks saw immediately that Network Marketing was a powerful, even inspired, structure that would enable them to pursue and achieve their dreams of business ownership and personal and financial freedom—regardless of their background.

WHERE HIGH-TECH MEETS HIGH-TOUCH

Throughout the 1980s, as Network Marketing companies came and went, the global concept of Network Marketing developed and grew. It was refined through trial and error, success and failure. Innovative products and new ways of doing business became more evident.

Technology has always been a driving force behind the industry. The 1950s Network Marketing distributor made good use of the car and phone. Thanks to these tools, distributors could easily hold in-home meetings and be in constant touch with new prospects.

A decade later, as the mimeograph machine was replaced by the modern copier, a whole new era of written communication opened up. Network Marketers could now easily create or reproduce everything from distributor applications, product information, company announcements, newsletters and direct mail packages—all with the touch of a button.

At no time in the industry's history, however, has technology had the tremendous impact that we have witnessed in the 1980s. Computer technology became affordable and understandable for just about everyone. (It's hard for me to imagine how a Network Marketing company back in the 1950s kept track of all their orders and commissions without them.) Even businesses with small budgets could afford a computer. At the very least, small businesses could get help from a third-party data processing service.

Low-cost airfare reduced the factors of time and distance even more, and Network Marketers were flying to meetings across their countries—and continents. In the 1980s, you could build a national, even an international Network and still maintain the all-important personal touch so necessary for success in this business. You've heard the phrase "Around the World in Eighty Days?" Well, thanks to fax machines, cellular phones, and teleconferencing, it's more like eighty *seconds*.

In each of these instances, Network Marketers were among the first to use these services and equipment. The industry has truly pioneered the use and refinement of many of the advances in technology that we take for granted today.

That brings us up to date. Next, let's look at where the industry is today.

CHAPTER FIVE

There's No Time Like The Present

Network Marketing is one of the world's fastest-growing methods of marketing and distribution. It's growing at a rate of between ten and fifteen percent per year, in or out of the broad economic cycle of recession and expansion during the past five years.

Today, there are an estimated fifteen to twenty million people participating in Network Marketing around the world. With the extraordinary growth of Network Marketing in Canada, Mexico, Australia, the Pacific Basin, the Far East, and Europe, this number could easily double by the turn of the century.

JUST TO GIVE YOU AN IDEA

According to the industry's resource center for Europe, MLM International (based in London England), Europe is now competing with Asia as the premier growth area for Network Marketing.

The European continent has over 800 million people with a high percentage of these being part of an affluent middle class. The Eastern Block and Mediterranean regions offer huge potential for Network Marketing as these highly educated populations cry out for business opportunities.

The United Kingdom is now an entry point for many overseas companies coming into the European marketplace. Its English speaking population is culturally diverse, providing an exceptional testing ground for any company planning to launch on the continent. And lately, the press in the United Kingdom has given some of the most positive support in the world to the concept of Network Marketing. With the U.K. having under one hundred companies and less than 300,000 people currently involved in the industry, the potential for growth is immense.

If we look at Europe as a whole, the potential for growth is even greater than immense. In the United States, 4% of their population of 270 million currently participate in a Network Marketing opportunity. Should the European population embrace the industry to the same extent, 4% of 800 million people is... potential for growth beyond comprehension.

Needless to say, the Europeans are very excited about their future as Europe appears to be positioned to play a key role in the Global expansion of Network Marketing in the 1990s and well beyond.

Network Marketing is also being embraced with open arms by the Aussies. While the world may recognize Australia for their kangaroos, koala bears and Crocodile Dundee, none of these are as visible to Australians as Network Marketing—which is growing faster than a lemon-scented Gum tree.

According to Spectrum Marketing, Australia's independent MLM resource center (based in Victoria), at a rough "guesstimate," Australia has around 450,000 distributors representing 150 Network Marketing companies with probably more than half representing the top five.

Annual sales are estimated at about $1.5 billion and are growing at about twenty percent a year. And they say that only about ten to fifteen percent of their 17 million plus population has even been *exposed* to the possibilities of Network Marketing. Sounds like the land "down-under" is a "ground floor" dream come true for the entrepreneur at heart.

Slightly further afield in South Coast Asia, Network Marketing is exploding. Indonesia, Thailand and Malaysia are thriving with activity, as are Japan, Korea and the Philippines. Even mainland China and its one billion plus people is about to experience its first taste of Network Marketing.

The small island of Taiwan is a strong example of the fast growing acceptance of Network Marketing throughout many parts of Asia.

There are 18.5 million people packed on this little (13,885 miles—a bit larger than the U.S. states of Maryland and Delaware combined) hot bed of entrepreneurial energy situated a short one hundred miles across the Formosa Strait from the mainland Republic of China.

The following figures for 1992 about the island's Network Marketing sales industry come from Taiwan's Fair Trade Committee. (Figures are in U.S. dollars.)

- Total sales volume was over $850 million

- As of April, 1992, Taiwan had 271 Network Marketing companies and 1.18 million independent distributors (6.4 percent of the population).

- 81% of all distributors were part-time.

- The average part-time distributor income was approximately $1,140

- The average full-time distributor income was approximately $3,400.

Pretty exciting, isn't it? The international growth of this industry makes the greatest opportunity in the history of the world just keep getting greater.

NETWORK MARKETING MAKES AND THE WORLD TAKES

I mentioned earlier how many new uses for the emerging technologies were pioneered by Network Marketers. What is perhaps even more revealing is how many major consumer trends were spearheaded by Network Marketing enterprises.

It wasn't long ago that vitamin and mineral supplementation was a concern for only a small percentage of the health-conscious population. Forty years ago, pioneering nutritional Network Marketing companies began to champion food supplements to the general public. Today, vitamins are a standard supermarket item. What's more, these early Network Marketing companies were leaders in offering *all-natural* formulations, a claim made today by every leading manufacturer.

There are many other examples. In the field of weight-loss, the "diet-in-a-can" phenomenon began in Network Marketing. Network Marketing pioneered environmentally-safe packaging, and "natural," products free of preservatives and artificial ingredients. Network Marketing has been instrumental in raising the public awareness on all of these innovations—long before it was fashionable. The small, in-home water filtration business exploded into a multi-billion dollar industry as a result of Network Marketing companies.

How about long-distance telephone service?

Can you remember when AT&T was the only game in town? Well, over three million customers were taken away from AT&T by Network Marketers representing Sprint and MCI, and there are thousands more "reaching out and touching someone" new every day!

In almost every field imaginable, innovations are being successfully brought to market by Network Marketers around the globe.

Why? Great question!

One big reason is money.

THE HIGH COST OF NEW PRODUCTS

The cost of bringing a new product to market is astronomical. Research and development costs are only the beginning. Millions soon grow to tens, even hundreds of millions for the most modest of new product introductions.

Did you know that the marketing tests for a single new product, just to see if it will sell in ten or twenty stores, can cost upwards of a million dollars or more? Expenses add up: free case samples, merchandising displays, warehouse slotting fees, broker-wholesaler-jobber commissions and incentives, co-op advertising, and couponing. And this list doesn't include expenses for a whole new production line back at the factory, sales costs, new packaging, inventory, regional TV, radio and newspaper advertising, and much more.

Is it any wonder that the little guys have been priced right out of the market? (By "little guys" I mean companies with less than a couple of hundred million dollars in annual sales.) It's a game only the super-rich corporations can afford to play.

Do you know that giants like General Mills require a minimum of $20 million or more of sales to make just one product viable? Or how about the cost of advertising: A thirty-second Super Bowl ad costs a whopping $900,000! Do you have any idea how many millions of dollars McDonalds spent to get you and I to hum, "You deserve a break today?" Hundreds of millions!

Now if you had a great new product or service and didn't happen to have $10 million lying around to bring it to market, what would you do? If you were smart you'd consider Network Marketing.

That's why our industry has such a phenomenal track

record of offering superior, innovative, state-of-the-art products and services. You see, not every great invention or new product idea comes from the rich multi-national corporations. Truth is, most of them come from little guys and gals like you and me. Innovative ideas like personal hygiene products, home water filters, unique diet products, leading-edge membership services, gas-saving automotive devices, toys and insurance—just to name a few.

THE BIG GUYS

Did you know that Colgate-Palmolive and Gillette offer products through Network Marketing? So does Avon, the $3 billion cosmetics giant. Prudential is one of the world's largest insurance companies, but did you know that the A.L. Williams Corporation (now Primerica) sold more individual life insurance through Network Marketing than Prudential? How about Shaklee, Mary Kay Cosmetics, or the world's largest plastic-housewares company, Tupperware? They're Network Marketers, too.

And don't think this is just a North American phenomenon. Amway, along with IBM and Mobil Oil, is one of the top ten fastest-growing foreign companies in Japan, with sales exceeding $1 billion. There are over 100 Network Marketing companies in Malaysia alone! And the new common-market Europe is already benefiting from foreign language editions of industry publications and books—just like this one.

Now, picture yourself way up in the executive dining room at AT&T and being the guy or gal who has to tell the chairman of the board about losing 3 million long distance customers. Or how about sitting in the President's penthouse office in the Prudential Building in Boston, explaining how A. L. Williams, after only ten years, sold more individual life insurance than you did. Do you think those guys are interested in what's happening down here at the grass-roots level? You bet!

And with the high cost of new product introductions and the constant pressure to discover new markets, more major corporations are turning to Network Marketing than ever before.

THE LEGACY OF FRANCHISING

It wasn't long ago that franchising was the fastest-growing industry in the U.S.

When franchising began over thirty years ago, people questioned its viability and credibility just as they do now with Network Marketing. Today franchising is well-integrated into our global economy—in America alone, one-third of all goods and services are sold through franchises!

I spoke about franchises earlier and mentioned the

fact that a moderately successful franchise costs the buyer an average of $85,000 to purchase. When you contrast that to owning your own Network Marketing business, you'll see why Network Marketing has become one of the world's fastest-growing methods for distributing products and services.

NETWORK MARKETING VERSUS FRANCHISES

There are other differences between Network Marketing and franchising. In Network Marketing, you don't have employees. You and everyone you sponsor into the business are independent contractors. This distinction saves you, the business owner, a lot of money and a ton of headaches.

Another major benefit of a Network Marketing business is that you choose who you want to work with. You are not forced to sponsor people you don't really *want* to work with because you *need* to.

Network Marketers work when they want, where they want (usually out of their home which offers significant tax advantages), and how they want. There are no standard hours or a retail location that must be opened according to schedule. And remember, Network Marketers are volunteers. You're not obligated to do anything. So how you work your business is completely up to you.

Another difference is the power of "geometric progression." Billionaire J. Paul Getty once said that he'd rather have one percent of the efforts of one hundred people, than one hundred percent of his own. Does that make sense to you? I hope so, because it's one of the biggest benefits of owning a Network Marketing business.

As you bring people into your Network and train them to achieve success, the company you're with pays you for those efforts. Soon, you'll have a growing Network of independent business builders like yourself, each person being paid on the movement of goods and services throughout the Network.

Let's say you sponsor five people into the business. Those five each do the same thing. How many people is that? Well, now you have three levels: you, the five you originally sponsored, and twenty-five new people. Now, if each of those twenty-five brings in five more new people....

Well, you see what's going to happen. An organization of hundreds, even thousands can be built in a relatively short period of time.

Of course, not everyone you or your people sponsor into the business will be a serious business builder. Far from it. The beauty is *that they don't have to be.* You only need a handful of serious people in your Network to be a big success in this business.

RESIDUAL INCOME

I spoke about residual income back in Chapter Three also, but it is so important, it deserves another mention.

For most people, residual income is an elusive dream. If you weren't born rich, don't have the talent or even "luck" to be an inventor, musician or performer, or don't have the good fortune to have a half-million dollars lying around to invest in stocks or real estate, the door to residual income is essentially closed to you.

As far as I know, the *only* place where ordinary people can make extraordinary money is in a successful Network Marketing business.

Now we all have a very personal definition of what it means to be wealthy. One person's goal of a few extra thousand dollars is another person's outrageous fortune.

But enduring, steadily increasing wealth is possible in Network Marketing. I personally know many millionaires, and many more "thousandaires," who are earning residual income after only one to four years in their own Network Marketing business. What's more, the Network Marketing concept is immediately appreciated by highly successful people. They know the value of residual income. That's why they can see the possibilities of a part-time or full-time Network Marketing career right away.

That's one reason why more and more professional and managerial people are entering the industry. Here's another.

Business researchers estimate that over the next five years, as many as thirty percent of all middle managers will be out of work, thanks to computers, corporate cost-cutting, and improved management/employee systems and communications. According to the latest projections, the number of people who need to hold down two or more jobs will double in the next five years.

WORKING WOMEN

I'm certain you're aware of the tremendous increase in the number of women entering and re-entering the workplace. Although many things have changed in the corporate world, women still earn less than their male counterparts—for American women, about $0.62 for every dollar a man earns. Sex discrimination is especially true in managerial positions where the "glass ceiling" prevents women from getting to the top of traditionally male-dominated industries.

There isn't any ceiling for women in Network Marketing.

Sixty-five percent or more of Network Marketers are women. The reason for this is not simply the growing pressure to become a two-income family and earn more money. Women are attracted to Network Marketing for two reasons.

1. There are no barriers of sex, education or experience in this industry.

2. Network Marketing is the ideal industry for most women. Let me explain why.

Network Marketing is a "nurturing" business. It's built by caring about others and encouraging them to succeed. That's why the most successful group of people entering Network Marketing are female teachers. Combine their skill of teaching with their ability to recommend products and services, and you've got a dynamite marriage for success.

The fact is that women are also better talkers and explainers than men. Now please, don't get upset with me. This *is* a fact. Researchers at the Harvard Preschool Program studied little boys and girls and found that only sixty-eight percent of what came out of a little boy's mouth were words. The other thirty-two percent was just noise. You know, "uh," "mmm," spurts, pops, and motor sounds like, "brrrruuum," "varooom," and "buh-buh-buh." On the other hand, every sound the little girls made were actual words!

And I love this one. That same survey found that the average man speaks approximately 12,500 words per day. How many for the average woman? 25,000!

Let me tell you a story that illustrates this.

I was consulting with a business friend of mine in his home-office when his five-year-old son burst through the door. We were having an important meeting, but the little boy interrupted anyway.

"Daddy, daddy, I've gotta ask you an important question."

His father was very short with him. They had a rule at their house that Daddy was not to be disturbed when he was in a business meeting. So, my friend told him, "Son, you've interrupted me. I'm very busy. Why don't you ask your Mother?"

The little boy looked up at his dad and replied, "But Daddy, I just don't want to know that much about it."

Most women love to talk and share. And the Network Marketing industry loves to reward talkers—not undercover agents!

You know, as I travel around the world, I meet a tremendous number of successful couples who have built large and prosperous Network Marketing businesses. One interesting thing I find is that many of these successful enterprises were begun by the women. Once the men saw how great the business was (and especially after their wives started making more money than they were), the men quit their jobs and joined them. It happens all the time.

SUCCESS STORIES

I've given you a number of reasons why Network Marketing is growing so rapidly, and I've listed a number of corporate success stories. But Network Marketing is not about the success of corporations. It's about the success of people just like you.

Remember "Jim's Story" in the beginning of the book? Well, I have listened to literally thousands of success stories just like Jim's. Each is unique, yet they all have something in common: The men, women, and families involved have dramatically changed their lives through Network Marketing.

Rags to riches stories are always impressive. I've known people who were broke, bankrupt, who had no hope for the future. Yet, in spite of all that, they began their Network Marketing business, and in a few short years, emerged earning an extraordinary income. Incomes of $15,000 to $50,000 per month are more than possible in Network Marketing. People are accomplishing that every day. The truth is, if you've never made anywhere near that kind of money, it's pretty hard to believe, especially when the person making that money began their business working part-time. But in this business, even if it sounds too good to be true, *it really can be!*

Here's the truth: *You* can earn $2,500, $5,000 or $10,000 a month and more in Network Marketing with the right product and company in one to four years of part-time (*not* just sometime) effort. It's a proven fact. Thousands and thousands of people are doing it this very minute. I know. I've met lots of them and I'm meeting more and more everyday. And do you want to know something? They're not any smarter or better than you are. They just know something you don't know—yet!

One more thing. Money isn't everything. I know we speak about money a great deal in Network Marketing. That's because in today's world, money is *required*. You cannot focus on owning your own life or making a difference in the lives of others if you're broke and can't pay the rent. In a recent survey by *Money Magazine*, forty percent of their readers felt that an unexpected bill of $1,000 would be "a big problem." As a whole, Americans save only five percent of their income. Twenty percent of all Americans have absolutely nothing set aside. Financially or otherwise, that's not freedom.

But for me, and for thousands and thousands of Network Marketers, additional income is only one of the benefits of this business. Number one on the list is personal growth.

Network Marketing literally transforms people's lives. Something special happens to people as they grow and especially when they directly contribute to the success of others. Years drop away from their faces as self-centered concerns disappear. This business offers the opportunity to master so many valuable life skills: listening, communication, public speaking, business, organization, friendship, finance, teaching, coaching, and more. And when you see a man or woman, who six months before had zero self-esteem, get up in front of a room of people and speak with enthusiasm and confidence—well, that's when you realize just how powerful this business really is.

No matter who or where you are in life, Network Marketing can make you better. In fact, I say that being the best in this business makes you the best in life!

Now, let's review some of the reasons for Network Marketing's tremendous success:

A SUMMARY OF SUCCESS

Network Marketing is today's fastest-growing method for distributing new products and services:

1. It's a $20 billion plus industry growing at ten to fifteen percent per year.

2. More than half of all American households purchase goods and services from Network Marketers.

3. It's a worldwide phenomenon that's rapidly becoming a leading export for some countries.

4. It has a proven track record of success with multi-billion dollar companies.

---

5. It's a perfect way to market innovative new products and services.

6. It's the most cost-effective way to bring these products to market.

7. It offers all the benefits of franchising for a fraction of the cost.

8. It's the best way for average people to earn residual income.

9. It offers "white-collar" people a viable alternative in a shrinking workplace.

10. It's perfect for working women.

11. And perhaps the best reason of all: Network Marketing is the best way in the world for ordinary people to achieve lasting, extraordinary success in life.

For all of the above reasons, Network Marketing is being called "The Wave of the Future."

So, what about the future? Where is this industry going?

That's what I want to share with you next.

CHAPTER SIX

Stepping
Into The Future

"America's greatest import is people. Yet Americans have not even begun to experience the real potential of their fantastic human resource mix, which will be their competitive edge in the global economy as we move toward the next millennium." * — Megatrends 2000

When I speak at a Network Marketing company's convention, I stand up in front of the room and look out at hundreds of men and women from every conceivable background. I see people from Canada and Mexico, South America and Europe, Asia and Malaysia, Korea and Japan, Australia and New Zealand.

---

* John Naisbitt and Patricia Aburdene, *Megatrends 2000* (New York: William Morrow and Company, Inc., 1990).

There are people in the audience who have never had a job before, and some who experienced the ultimate failure—bankruptcy! I've met a small-business owner in an audience who lost everything to a devastating fire. I've met truck drivers, homemakers, retired engineers, people from every walk of life.

Do you know what I see the most when I scan all those eager faces?

The future. Quite simply, *you* are the future of Network Marketing.

You see, Network Marketing is a "melting pot" itself. It's filled with people from every corner of the globe. All types of sizes, shapes, colors and histories. And, you know something? Even though everyone is different, they all are the same—they all dream of being the best they can possibly be.

There is no prejudice in Network Marketing. None! That's one of the reasons I love it so! Everyone is of such common mind and purpose—there's no time or room for prejudice.

THE BABY BOOMERS

Here's some interesting American history. Every nation has its history of change and expectations of future trends. So as I explain mine to you, think about (and perhaps get a better understanding of) where your country has come from, where it is today and most importantly—where it's going. You may recognize that many of us are headed in the same direction—towards a more interactive, inter-related world and global economy.

If you were born in the U.S. between 1946 and 1964, you may have a bigger impact on Network Marketing than you realize. As you may be aware, that was the age of the "Baby Boom"—an era responsible for creating the single most influential socioeconomic force in American society. Today there are almost seventy-six million "boomers" across America, with the bulk of them battling mid-life crises and the responsibilities of raising families.

The success and continued expansion of Network Marketing in the United States lies with the buying power of this group. Give these people what they want, and you have *the greatest opportunity in the history of the world* at your command.

Let me explain.

"WHAT A DRAG IT IS, GETTING OLD..."

It's a little hard to believe, for those of us who grew up with the Rolling Stones, that Mick Jagger is almost fifty years old. For that matter, it seems like most Boomers are having difficulty with the passing of time.

The image of "looking and feeling young" is as important to this group as it ever has been. And boy, are marketers aware of this.

You name it, boomers have bought it. From Lean Cuisine to brewed decaf, pocket transistor radios, home computers, microwaves, BMWs, condominiums... the list goes on and on.

Anybody who ever gave the boomers and their parents what they wanted—from the early 1940s to the present—became fabulously successful. In the forties, before the "boom," a small family-owned company called Gerber had the bright idea of producing prepared baby food to save American mothers precious time and trouble. In 1940, that entire industry filled 270 million jars. In 1955, Gerber alone sold 1.5 billion jars of strained peaches, pears and peas!

How would you like to have a dime for every "slinky" and "hula hoop" sold through the fifties and sixties?

Imagine what would have happened if you were constructing new elementary schools in the mid-1950s? In 1957, there were more elementary schools built than in the previous twelve years combined!

Ever heard of Bill Levitt? He created the first, mass-produced housing development (Levittown, PA) to give boomer families affordable homes.

From a small, Philadelphia TV program, Dick Clark

created American Bandstand to give boomers what they wanted in music and entertainment. He created a mega-million dollar entertainment empire out of that, and he's been doing it ever since.

In another part of the country, Ray Kroc created McDonalds—fast, affordable food for people on the run.

With few exceptions, the vast majority of goods and services offered today are made and sold—directly or indirectly—to boomer families. And the power of the cash register is the most formidable force in contemporary Western society.

Most of today's boomers are in their forties now. They are starting to reach the peak of their careers, either settling down into executive positions, or switching to completely different jobs. They are economically, socially, and politically very powerful. They are the leaders of America's next century which, I might add, is only a few short years away!

There's one more thing about this group of people that may interest you.

THE AGE WAVE

Dr. Ken Dychtwald has written a fascinating book called *The Age Wave*, which talks about one of the most exciting ideas I've ever read. It's subtitled, "How the Most Important Trend of our Time Will Change Your

Future." On the front cover it also says, "If you expect to live to the year 2000, you need to read this book!"

What's going to happen in the year 2000?

By then, according to Dychtwald, two things will happen. The boomers will be over fifty years old. Once that happens, they will combine with the second-largest segment (the 50+ generation) to form the largest single cluster of people in American society. This is what he calls the "age wave."

Now, if we as global Network Marketers, can tap into their concerns and needs early on, we can also be successful. Remember, the buying power of this group will probably be the most significant influence on Network Marketing in America for years to come.

So, what are their concerns?

Truth: This generation has lived through Watergate. They are turned off by false advertising and appreciate straightforward honesty.

Quality: This generation has also learned a thing or two from their parents. They are buying smarter, choosing products which will be around for years.

Service: Most boomers typically do not have a lot of time to waste waiting for bad service. The shorter the wait—whether it's 24-hour tellers, drive-throughs, one-hour photo shops or whatever—the better.

Entertainment: This generation also plays harder than their parents did. Just look at their toys: compact disc players, stereo TVs, hot tubs, jet skis, 4-wheel drive vehicles.... They aren't "couch potatoes." Not this group!

Health: It's been said that boomers will be content to feel and look fifty, by the time they're 100—and not a day sooner! Because of that, boomers have tried, and will continue to try, everything under the sun to reverse the clock. Everything from Slim Fast, jogging and Soloflex machines to liposuction and plastic surgery. This group has tried it all.

Freedom: Most importantly, *do not* tell these people what to do. They demand a choice!

Money: They like to spend it. Budgets are out— "How do I make more money?"—is in!

And what offers all of these things, and more? Only one thing I know of: Network Marketing, the wave of the future.

THE SIGN OF THE TIMES

However, before we can prepare for the future, and everything it will bring, we need to be in the right frame of mind. I've got a great story which illustrates this.

In the late 1800s, a famous bishop from the Midwest was travelling the United States speaking to groups of religious and academic leaders. During his journey, he received an invitation for dinner from the president of a small, highly-regarded and progressive Western college, and graciously accepted.

The bishop was warmly greeted, and was treated to a fine formal meal at the president's home. Then, after dinner, the prominent faculty members gathered around the great man to discuss the future over brandy and cigars.

"Sir, what do you think the future holds for mankind?" asked one faculty member.

The bishop became quite stern, the joviality vanishing from his face.

"My good man, the future is bleak," he replied. "In my opinion, we have discovered all there is to discover, created all there is to create, invented all there is to invent, and now we are on a path of decline and self-destruction."

Silence smothered the room.

Finally, the president of the college (who was also a professor of physics) spoke up.

"Bishop," he began apologetically, "I beg to disagree. I cannot believe that we are on the eve of destruction. I sense that we have just begun an era of great progress such as our world has never seen before. I mean no offense, sir, but I am convinced things we have only dreamed of today will surely become real tomorrow."

The bishop was astonished. He was not accustomed to being challenged, even politely.

"What dreams do you imagine we will witness?" he demanded.

"Sir, someday I think man shall learn to fly like the birds."

"You must be mad," the bishop bellowed. "Flight is reserved for the angels."

With that, he stormed out of the room, putting an end to the evening's discussion.

You see, what I didn't tell you was that the bishop's last name was Wright. A couple of decades later, his two sons Orville and Wilbur, made the dream of flight real on the windswept salt marshes of Kitty Hawk.

It's easy for us to laugh at the bishop's pessimistic outlook. After all, we have the advantage of looking into the past and seeing a whole chain of innovations—the airplane, light bulb, telephone, automobile.... The bishop would probably have protested just as loudly at the idea of a man walking on the moon, or the idea of a letter sent cross-country in the blink of an eye.

You see, the bishop, with all his knowledge, wasn't

open to the idea of change. He was stuck in his ways, and refused to shift his point of view.

Can you imagine what would happen if the rest of us had that same attitude?

A CHANGING AMERICA

Since the birth of the United States, many things have happened—and are continuing to happen. Change is all around us, and today our world is changing faster than ever before.

At the time of our story about the bishop, the United States was primarily an agricultural society. Back then, close to ninety percent of the population was responsible for producing one hundred percent of its food.

By the latter part of the 1800s, it had become an industrial society. Carnegie, Rockefeller, Getty and the other great tycoons of business transformed their nation into an industrial powerhouse. During the 1920s, 30s, and 40s, the United States was at the peak of its industrial manufacturing power. It was responsible for producing fifty percent of the entire world's industrial goods. American steel, ships, machines, cars, tools, and planes, spilled out all over the world.

In a little less than one hundred years, this nation bolted like lightning through the three major eras of modern times: The Age of Agriculture, The Age of Industry, and today, the Age of Information and Service.

Just to compare how far it's come, today only three percent of the people in America produce an astonishing 120 percent of the food it needs! Although the industrial production has dropped off a little, it's still twenty-five percent of the entire world's industrial goods.

Resistance to change in this day and age is understandable. Never before have things moved so quickly and in such quantum leaps. Just look at what's happening around the globe: The Berlin Wall is down and the Pacific Rim is exploding in a frenzy of free enterprise. Democracy and capitalism were elected by popular demand in Eastern Europe! Look at the progress in South Africa and the rapidly changing landscape of what used to be called the Soviet Union.

GOING WITH THE FLOW

The 1960s attitude of "go with the flow" was pretty good advice after all. Look what's happening to the American farmer today. Or the steel and auto workers, faced with the loss of their jobs due to robots. Flexibility is the key to success in today's fluctuating marketplace.

Any progressive society must be fully committed to the dynamic transformation to the Age of Information and Service. With very rare exceptions, any country, any industry or any person swimming upstream against this tidal wave of the future is risking their own and their family's security.

Where is Network Marketing in this picture?

Right where you'd expect it to be. On the leading edge. The essence of Network Marketing is *information* and *service*. In fact, the closer you look at this industry and the trends shaping our world, the more profoundly you realize how perfect and powerful it is!

Like I've said before, having the right attitude is the key. Unless we open our minds to the idea of change, we won't be able to act upon it. As the story about the bishop shows, we could be standing on the brink of a historic moment, method or service which could change our lives forever—and still not see it stretched out before us.

Are you going to be content enough to let the future pass you by, while others—like the Wright brothers— try to seize it with all their energy?

Are you ready to make an impact on your future? On the future of others? On the future of Network Marketing? On the future of your country? On the future of your world?

Fantastic! Let me share with you an idea.

Sharing The Dream

So, my friends, do you remember how we began this book?

Do you remember the story of the powerful industrialist who captured all those rare and beautiful animals, and how he manipulated them into trading their freedom and their future for food?

Do you remember the little poem by Shel Silverstein, and how I asked you if this book could reveal to you a magic carpet...

> ...that could lift you over all your fences and
> whiz you through the air
> to health and wealth and happiness,
> if you just tell it where.

Would you let it take you
where you've never gone before
Or would you buy some drapes to match
and use it on your floor?

What have you decided—is it a rug or is it a magic carpet?

If you think Network Marketing could possibly be your magic carpet, then here's an idea I'd like to share with you: Think about where you would like it to take you.

How do you do that?

YOUR DREAM CAREER

Here's an exercise I conduct in my seminars that helps people reveal their dreams.

I want you to assume that you're free to design the perfect career for yourself. Remember, you're on a magic carpet that will take you anywhere you want to go. There's no place or room here for doubt. We're talking about your dreams—not your fears.

Ask yourself: What are the five most important qualities I would want in my perfect dream career?

Now don't be concerned whether or not you can have all of these. Don't try to list them in any kind of order either, and don't think these are the *only* qualities you can have. This is just a start.

You know what might help? Let me share with you some of the qualities I want in my perfect dream career.

1. Money. In our world, money is a must. How much money? That depends on what you want and how much you believe you're worth.

For me, I see money as a tool that enables me to function freely within my world and accomplish all the things I dream of—and I have some pretty big dreams! So I want enough money to make me financially free to be, do, have and contribute all that I want.

Now I know that money can't buy or guarantee me happiness. I also know that not having money doesn't guarantee me happiness either! So I look at it this way. I do what I do because I love to do it, and because I believe it's of value to others. If what we do is of value, why not expect and accept abundance in return? We deserve it!

2. Creativity. I love bringing things into existence that weren't there before. Creativity is my key to personal growth and empowering others. It's my vehicle of self-expression, of putting who I am and what I do out into the world.

3. Acknowledgment. This is flat-out one of my most important needs, both as a receiver and a giver. I want to make a difference in people's lives and acknowledgment is my measuring rod.

And very few things give me more satisfaction than sharing my abundance and prosperity with those I love and treasure. Those people that are making a big difference in my life as well. It's true that to give is better than to receive. As far as I'm concerned, acknowledgment makes our world go 'round.

4. Trust. Integrity, loyalty, friendship... all of these come under the heading of trust for me. I want to trust people because I want people to trust me. I only want to be in relationships where everyone is trusting of each other. It's a risk, I know—but it's the only place that I know of where my mind is free to create!

5. Contribution. Like I said earlier, I want to make a BIG difference in people's lives. I feel the best about myself when I am helping bring out the best in others. Contribution and service are big parts of my purpose—and *living my purpose* is the single most important quality my perfect career must provide!

Now, I have other ingredients in my perfect career as well. Fun, what I do must be fun. Action, I've got to be in action to be happy. Freedom, time to be with my family and friends. The list is endless, but these five qualities are the first ones that came to my mind. What are yours?

What I'm going to ask you to do, in just a moment, is to write down five qualities you want from your perfect dream career. Then, after you list each quality, ask yourself these two questions:

1. What does that *mean* to me?

2. What does that *provide* for me? What will that *give* me?

It's best to be brief, and again, don't feel that these won't change. They may. In fact, I suggest you use a pencil so you can change them whenever you want. Ready? Good, let's begin:

What are five qualities I want in my perfect dream career?

1. _____

   _____

2. _____

   _____

3. _____

   _____

4. _____

_____

5. _____

_____

What do these qualities mean to me?

1. _____

_____

2. _____

_____

3. _____

_____

4. _____

_____

5. _____

_____

What will each of these qualities provide for me?

1. _____

_____

2. _____

_____

3. _____

_____

4. _____

_____

5. _____

_____

Great. Now take a moment to carefully look back over your list. Please do that now.

What do you think? How does reading those things make you feel? Remember, there's no room for doubt here. We're talking about your dreams—not your fears.

When I look back over my list, I get pretty inspired. Just imagine what it would be like to work a business that offered you all the qualities you believe to be important to you! Do you think that would get you out of bed in the morning? You bet!

Now, there are two reasons these five ingredients are so important.

First, as I explained in the first chapter of my book, *Being The Best You Can Be In MLM* ("Your Goals and Purpose"), mastery in any endeavor is only ten percent knowing "how," and ninety percent knowing "why." With these five key ingredients, you've got a great grasp on the "why" of your perfect dream career.

The second reason is that now you can contact the person who gave you this copy of *The Greatest Opportunity In The History Of The World* to schedule a time to sit down with him or her and talk about your list together. Take a look at their opportunity. Can it provide for you the things you want most in your life and your work?

I cannot tell you how many people call and write to thank me (and remember, acknowledgment was one of the five on my list!) for the part in *Being The Best You Can Be In MLM* that had them focus on their goals and purpose *before* they did anything else in this business. This helps people who are considering a Network Marketing career (like you) to get straight and clear about what they really want. It also enables the men and women who are sponsoring you into the business to make sure their opportunity is right for you—and that you are right for it.

There is simply no better way to begin in this business than understanding and believing in your "why."

THE SIX QUESTIONS

In all my years in this business, I've discovered that anyone who is considering a Network Marketing career must ask and receive answers for the following six questions in order for them to want to get started. In my first book I only listed five, but I've added another question because it's so important.

I want to share these with you now. I want you to be aware that these questions are within you as well, even if you don't realize they're there. You'll soon see how important they are. And I recommend that both you and your potential sponsor keep them in front of you when you meet to discuss your involvement in this business.

Here they are:

1. Is IT LEGAL?

I've spent a lot of time talking about this. Is Network Marketing legal? Yes. Is the company you are considering legal? Here's what to look for:

Look for a successful product or service with genuine value and a competitive price. Remember, this is a specialty products business, so expect to see high-quality products.

Does this mean that you shouldn't go with a company that introduces an innovative, never-seen-before product or service? No, it's just that the risk is greater. Knowing what will appeal to the public before it's proven successful is both a talent and a matter of luck. Do your best to test it out first to make sure it's something you really believe in and other people will want—then go for it. And remember, you've got to love your product. Enthusiasm is eighty percent of your business, and the key to enthusiasm lies in the last four letters, IASM: **I Am Sold Myself!**

Look for a company that pays commissions only on the sales of products, *not* for the act of recruiting or sponsoring. Also, look for a company that emphasizes retail sales as well. Moving products and services to the end consumer is an important part of any successful business.

Look for a company that does not require a substantial investment to participate. You'll need a starter kit and initial product inventory, which can be a significant amount if your goals are high and you plan to be very aggressive in building your business. However, make sure that's *your choice*—and not a requirement.

While I'm on the subject of a sales kit, look closely at the sales aids or support materials the company provides to assist you in building your business. The quality of a company's sales aids is usually a good indication of the quality of the company itself.

Look for a company that does not misrepresent your earning potential. There are lots of claims of outrageous fortunes to be made in Network Marketing. Good companies only use conservative figures. Be cautious of ads and individuals that say you'll be making $50,000 in three months.

And look for a company that encourages distributors to be actively supporting, managing and training their people. This is not just a legal concern, it's just good sense to make sure you'll get the best support available for your success.

2. IS IT SIMPLE TO DO?

The key to success in this business is "duplication." If you can clearly grasp the opportunity and how to do it, so will the people you offer it to—and that's what you want.

Don't be put off if you don't understand the complexities of the compensation plan. Truth is, I know many top leaders in this business who don't fully understand theirs! As long as you can see how you will reach the various achievement levels, that's fine. And remember, in this business you can earn while you learn.

3. IS IT FUN?

Just look at the other people who are already involved. If they look like they haunt houses for a living, consider another company. Most won't. You can have more fun in this business than you ever imagined possible. And the truth is, the longer you're in it, the more fun it becomes!

4. CAN I REALLY MAKE MONEY?

This is simple enough. Look and see. Are others making money? Are people from varied backgrounds earning incomes for their efforts? Are new people who have been in the business a few weeks to a few months excited about their business and how it's growing?

Yes, it will likely take a considerable amount of time and energy before you receive that first $5,000 or $10,000 a month bonus check—but the journey of a lifetime always starts with the first step.

So have your potential sponsor point to the successes of those who are making it work for them. Then ask yourself, "Can I do it too?"

What you really want here is to get a good idea of the

time and energy you'll need to achieve the income you desire. What others have done and are doing should answer that question for you.

5. WILL THEY HELP ME TO DO IT?

This is *so very* important. Ask what your potential sponsor will do to help, support and train you. Ask what the company provides for you as well. I think you'll find this is one area where Network Marketing outshines the rest of the business world. That's because we know our success depends on helping others!

Now will all this guarantee your success? No. There are no guarantees in this or any other business. There are no guarantees in life for that matter. One thing is for sure: No matter how this particular endeavor of yours turns out, by putting your heart and soul into being the best you can be, you will learn an incredible amount in the process. Think of the growing and highly effective "circle of influence" you will gain. Your personal resources which include your belief system, your abilities, your unique skills and desires—all will be enlarged and enhanced. Imagine as well your higher levels of self-confidence and business acumen. Everything about you will be bigger and greater—and just waiting to serve you in life's next opportunity. And what's really beautiful is that no matter what happens, nothing or no one can take these away from you. You own these forever!

What you'll learn in this business will change your life for the better and make it work bigger and bolder than ever before. That fact, my friends, is guaranteed!

6. Is Now The Right Time To Get Involved?

Well—is it?

This is the one you and only you can answer. The question is: How do you know if this is the right time for you?

Remember the story of Jim? He was the enthusiastic young man back in the beginning of the book who attended his friend's funeral and had a moving experience of what he *really* wanted out of life. Let's re-create that experience as an exercise, and use it to help you decide if now is the right time for you to get involved in a business of your own—a Network Marketing business of your own.

Here's what you do. In a moment, I'm going to ask you to sit back, take a deep breath and imagine yourself at a funeral. It's not sad at all. In fact, it's a real celebration. The person whose life everyone is gathered around to acknowledge was greatly admired, respected and deeply loved. A real personal and professional success. A person who made a positive difference in many people's lives. And that person *is you!*

Now, I ask you to take a deep breath, close your eyes and imagine that scene. Imagine a dear friend of yours standing, addressing the group and speaking about you and all you've accomplished. The people that you've touched, the unique differences that you've made. As soon as that image is rich in your mind, open your eyes and immediately begin writing down the things that person is saying about you.

(Just a note: Keep writing no matter what. There is no right or wrong thing to write here. If you lose your focus, just close your eyes, imagine the scene again and continue writing.)

_____

_____

_____

_____

_____

_____

_____

_____

_____

_____

_____

_____

_____

_____

_____

_____

_____

_____

_____

_____

_____

_____

_____

_____

_____

_____

_____

Hopefully you have unveiled some things about you and your dreams that you may have never realized before. Things you'd like to be remembered for, acknowledged and appreciated for contributing. I guess you could even call these things your legacy. Your unique mark on time and on other people that will forever make a difference.

Earlier I had you identify five of the key qualities you would want in your perfect dream career. You also learned the six questions you needed answered in order for you to say, "Yes," and get involved. And you now have a powerful, visual sense in writing as well, of how you want your life to turn out—your legacy.

So now ask yourself... "Is my current career fulfilling what is really important to me? Am I living each day with meaning and purpose? Am I creating for myself the legacy I have envisioned? Is what I'm doing and how I'm doing it what I really want from life?"

If you answer yes, then I'm sure you're very happy with yourself and what you do. This exercise, then, has been a great affirmation of your chosen path.

However, if you feel a void, change is inevitable. Either you change your *attitude* about what you do or you change *what* you do.

Know that change does not always have to be painful or drastic. It can be subtle and quite gradual. One thing is for sure, though: Change is both inevitable and constant! And the risks one must take to explore the possibilities of it are proportionate!

So, if you're not becoming everything you want to be, doing everything you want to do, and having everything you want to have in life—if you're not doing the things that are contributing to the legacy you have envisioned for yourself—then it might be time to explore other possibilities. Look to change! The cost can be very little compared to the possible gain. What's a good way to do that? It could be as simple as meeting with the person who gave you this book.

SHARING THE DREAM

If you're like most people in my seminars, these exercises have left you feeling strong, energized and creative. They're an empowering experience. As good as they are at bringing clarity and a sense of purpose to your dreams, there's still one thing missing: sharing.

A couple of thousand years ago, the Greek philosopher Plato said one of the most important things in all of human history: *"The truth is revealed in dialogue."*

All the insight and inspiration you get from compelling exercises, making lists of key qualities you value and even writing down your life's purpose mean little until you share them with another person. There's something very special about people getting together to share their dreams.

Sure, two heads are better than one—but it's much, much more than that. Network Marketing is a people to people business. Not simply because it uses word-of-mouth advertising to offer products and opportunities to others. A Network Marketing business is special because *it is the gift of sharing itself that makes it so powerful, satisfying and fulfilling.*

Whether over the phone, one-on-one in a coffee shop, or in a group, sharing ourselves is what this business is all about. When we share, we reveal a whole new dimension of ourselves and others. We grow closer. We honor each other. Through speaking and listening with integrity, we bring the truth that lives in our dreams to the surface of our lives.

The Chinese have a wonderful philosophy that goes something like this: "Once you have been given a gift of great value, you are obligated to share it with others." That's what the person who gave you this book is up to.

That's why they want to share their opportunity with you. They have an obligation to do so. It's their way of saying thanks while guaranteeing the continued flow of more good information back into their life.

Imagine the consequences if someone gave you a gift (in the form of information, a product or a service) that helped you improve the quality of your life and you chose not to share that gift with others. You refused to perpetuate its value and benefit to others. You didn't even give others the opportunity to learn about it so they could choose to either use it or pass on it!

Choosing to break that chain—that constant flow of hope, promise and truth that all of us need and benefit from—is not only selfish, it can be self-destructive.

Network Marketing has created a way for the both of you to be rewarded for this natural act of sharing. It's something we do all the time.

You and the person who gave you this copy of *The Greatest Opportunity In The History Of The World* have the good fortune to experience the power that comes from mutual sharing. You have a rare opportunity to sit down with each other and share your dreams. Once you do, I promise both of you will never quite be the same again.

While reading this book, if you found yourself thinking positively about the possibilities of your own Network Marketing business, my recommendation is that you contact the person who gave you this book *right now* and make an appointment as soon as possible. You both could gain a great deal by doing so.

EXERCISING ONE'S WISDOM

I can only hope that as a result of this book you feel more informed and much wiser when it comes to evaluating the possibilities and the realities of a Network

Marketing business of your own. If so, great! That was my purpose.

So let me now tell you one final story.

There was a wise man who was much beloved by the people of his country. There was also an evil Prince who hated the wise man for having the affection of the people while he, the Prince, did not. The Prince sought constantly to discredit the wise man. Finally, he hit upon a plan.

"Tomorrow," said the Prince, "when the wise man goes to the marketplace to talk to the people, I shall be there. I will hold a dove in my hand, and I will say, 'Wise Man! Tell me—this bird which I hold in my hand—is it alive or dead?' If he says it is dead, I will open my hand and let the bird fly away. If he says it is alive, I will crush the dove in my hand and let in fall to the ground, dead. Either way, I will have made the wise man appear a fool!"

The next day came, and the Prince was at the market-place before the wise man arrived. He waited patiently, and when the wise man appeared and began speaking, the Prince took the dove from its cage and raised his voice above the crowd.

"Wise Man!" he shouted, "I would ask you a simple question: This bird which I hold in my hand, is it alive or dead?"

The crowd grew silent, and all eyes turned toward the wise man. The wise man paused, looked first at the people and then at the Prince, and said: "That which you hold in your hand, *it is what you make of it.*"

Network Marketing is The Greatest Opportunity In The History Of The World! It can be your magic carpet to health and wealth and happiness, and to a life of success and fulfillment such as you have only dared dream possible.

My friends, it is possible. *It is also what you make of it!* And it all begins with the sharing of our dreams.

I'd like to acknowledge you for your willingness to be open and your desire to explore the truth. Thank you for the opportunity you've given me to share my dreams and for being *one of my one million friends*! I wish you the best that life has to offer. And remember...

You can fly, if you try!

Your friend,

ABOUT THE AUTHOR

"When I founded Millionaires in Motion in 1985," says John Kalench, "the Network Marketing industry had a very real need for a no-nonsense approach to education. Millionaires in Motion has come a long way in filling that gap."

A leading trainer, consultant and visionary for the Network Marketing industry, John Kalench was first introduced to Network Marketing in 1979. Over the next eight years, John built three highly profitable distributorships and was also the President, CEO and controlling stockholder in his own Network Marketing company.

In 1985, John was positioned atop a network of thousands of distributors nationwide. He created Millionaires in Motion (MIM) to provide specialized training programs for his network.

John's training programs were immediately embraced by his sales leaders throughout the country, and, in February of 1987, he decided to make MIM an independent training company for the entire Network Marketing industry. To meet this objective, MIM divorced itself from financial interest in any particular company—training and consulting would be its only business.

Since then, thousands of Network Marketing entrepreneurs have attended John's seminars and graduated from his workshops all over the world. Top sales leaders and company principals have also used his consulting expertise to better direct and expand their business strategies.

For two consecutive years, MIM received the President's award for training excellence from the MLMIA (Multi-Level Marketing International Association).

"Our mission is clear," says John. "We want you to think of us as your Global Ambassadors of Network Marketing."

JOHN KALENCH

*"True prosperity in MLM/Network Marketing
comes only when you love your industry
as much as you love your products and company."*

How to put the power of this book to work for you.

Everyone in your network should have a copy of **The Greatest Opportunity In The History of The World.** *A great prospecting tool, this fast-reading book establishes the truths and dispels the myths about the past, present and future of the Network Marketing industry.*

Currently available in English, German, Italian & Spanish.

Prospecting tools that keep working... and working... and working..

THE MASTER PROSPECTOR KIT

Imagine having 80 employees working for you 24 hours a day, 7 days a week—sharing the dream of network marketing with your prospects. That's exactly what you get in the Master Prospector Kit. Your kit includes 12 books, 12 audios, 6 videos, and a pack of 50 brochures—all based on the best-selling book, *The Greatest Opportunity in the History of the World,* by John Kalench.

These concise and informative tools present the network marketing in a professional light while addressing common misconceptions and myths. They are proven to dramatically increase your chances of sponsoring business builders—not just wholesale product users. Your guide to prospecting mastery (also included) shows you how to share the right piece with the right prospect at the right time. With a retail value of almost $300, you save nearly 60% by purchasing this powerful prospecting kit.

Order # 501SNM - $124.95

WARNING! DO NOT READ THIS!
Unless you're serious about building your business.

The Six-Week Action Course™ is a must if you:

- Want to be a part of a powerful, productive team
- Need to bring step-by-step clarity and focus to your business
- Desire a simple system for duplicating your success with others
- Wish to build camaraderie and synergy within your network
- Want to experience the rewards of working with responsible and accountable teammates
- Aspire to set and achieve goals higher than you've ever imagined
- Enjoy participating in a training program that is both fun and effective

The Six-Week Action Course™ is the most powerful team-building and training system available to network marketers today. Never before has there been a more effective program that combines the power of laser-like goal setting, specialized training, and structured team support.

The Six-Week Action Course™ is the most comprehensive system for building the network marketing business of your dreams—we guarantee it! Find out more, call one of our Action Course Tele-Coaches now! 1-800-388-1748. They'll answer your questions and tell you how you can get started—RISK FREE!
Order # 107ANM - $69.95
Quantity discounts available.

Other Best Selling Books
by John Kalench

Being The Best You Can Be in MLM. *If you could only read one book on the subject of network marketing, ask any successful sales leader and they'll tell you... "Read Being the Best You Can Be in MLM by John Kalench."* **$14.95** *U.S.*

17 Secrets of the Master Prospectors. *The most powerful principles and techniques used by the best in Network Marketing—all over the world. Contains Action Steps for mastery of each secret. It's like getting 17 books in one!* **$14.95** *U.S.*

Have you met these folks?

L.I.S.T.E.N.

If you haven't, you will! So be prepared by learning the six simple steps to answering these and all objections successfully.

Your L.I.S.T.E.N. program includes
- An entertaining audio tape capturing a lively discussion between three network marketing masters giving powerful responses to your most common objections.
- A 32-page workbook that allows you to review the written responses to these most common objections, and teaches you how to develop effective responses to objections unique to your company, product, or services.

You're never to old to fall in love... with objections.
Order your L.I.S.T.E.N.™ program today!

Order # 109ANM - $19.95   Quantity discounts available.

Audio/Video Home Study Programs by John Kalench

The Trilogy Series. Nothing beats a live presentation by John Kalench, so MIM has created this series of video/audio programs featuring John—live! Now you can bring John into your living room, to training meetings and to prospects. Ask us about our special "buy two, get one free" offer.

Your Fast Track To Network Marketing Success *(2 Audios/Video).* You only have one chance to give your business a fast start. Master the fast-start principles taught in John's live seminar by using these audio & video cassettes. **$39.95**$^{U.S.}$

If You Knew What I Know... A Two-Hour Live Interview With John Kalench *(2 Audios/Video).* This series is full of training tips and insights great for new prospects as well as for use as a training tool for your current business builders. **$39.95**$^{U.S.}$

Build Your Vision... *(Audio/Video).* John Kalench uses his heart-to-heart style to discuss the importance of vision in creating your successful Network Marketing business and the four cornerstones upon which that vision must be built. **$39.95**$^{U.S.}$

The Trilogy Special $79.90
Buy two programs and get the third FREE.
Save $39.95